Have You Seen The Wind?

Books by William F. Nolan

Short Fiction:
Impact 20
Alien Horizons
Wonderworlds
The Dandelion Chronicles
Things Beyond Midnight
Blood Sky
3 for Space
Helle on Wheels
Night Shapes
The Brothers Challis
Down the Long Night
Logan's Return
Dark Universe
Simply An Ending
Ships in the Night
With Marlowe in L.A.
Far Out
Wild Galaxy

Verse:
Hemingway: Last Days of the Lion (with nonfiction)
Dark Encounters
Have You Seen the Wind? (with fiction)

To Mark!
Dark best,
William F. Nolan

Have You Seen The Wind?

Selected Stories and Poems

by

William F. Nolan

BearManor Media
2003

Have You Seen The Wind?
© 2003 by William F. Nolan. All rights reserved.

For information, address:

BearManor Media
P. O. Box 750
Boalsburg, PA 16827

bearmanormedia.com

Cover design by John Teehan
Typesetting and layout by John Teehan

Published in the USA by BearManor Media
ISBN - 0-9714570-5-0
Library of Congress Control No. 2003100758

*This one is for
Christopher Conlon,
who knows why*

Table of Contents

Author's Introduction

If you write day in and day out for many years, you are driven to it. A strange personal chemistry demands the creative release found only in written words. Sure, you do it to make a living (and for the ego-boost), but you really do it because writing is the center of yourself and you have little choice in the matter. For you, to write is to breathe. Yes, it's agony some of the time, and it's hard work, and it's frustrating and demanding—but it's also sheer joy and triumph, and the process ultimately results in a deep sense of personal satisfaction. The writing is you. If you've been born to write, no one can keep you from it. The words, the images, the people are all inside of you, demanding release. And if you do get published, and you do reach those millions of minds out there in the world, then, by God, it's the greatest reward any person could ask for, and no other achievement in life can touch it.

Although I now have seventy-five books to my credit, *Have You Seen the Wind?* is unique: the first volume of mine to include both fiction and poetry under a single cover. In total, I've written over 180 short stories and approximately one hundred poems. For *William F. Nolan's Dark Universe* (published in 2001)—a fifty year career retrospective—I selected forty-one of my best tales. For *Have You Seen the Wind?* however, I made a fresh selection of stories that have never appeared in any Nolan book. These consist of three very recent tales (written after *Dark Universe* went to press), along with two others of slightly earlier vintage, plus a new story written just for this collection.

"Behind the Curtain" is almost entirely fictional. In it, I reproduce a conversation I had during a hospital visit last year. The climax, of course, is fiction. (I was never in a car crash; I went to the hospital for a totally different reason.)

"The Ex" (written in 1995 for a Nolan-themed issue of *Deathrealm*) is my only baseball tale. The story came to me in a dream, and thus became a nightmare put to paper. I'm always amazed at what my subconscious conjures up, and this is a prime example.

"Listening to Billy" is only partly fiction. It is based directly on a real-life event: the tragic murder/suicide of my next-door neighbors in Kansas City, Missouri, my hometown. Arthur and Adele (their real names) were like a second set of parents to me. Their horrific double death in 1948 was a shock that took me a full half-century to assimilate into my work. The sections involving Billy are fictional, but everything else in the story is true. And be warned: "Listening to Billy" is *not* a ghost story.

I wrote "In Real Life" for a recent Dennis Etchison anthology. Stark, savage, and uncompromising, it is an experiment in form and structure. I wanted to see how far I could push the stylistic envelope. As proof that my experiment was a success, this story was chosen for the Honor Roll in *The Year's Best Fantasy and Horror*. I try never to repeat myself, and this is truly one of a kind.

"Killing Charlie" was inspired by a story I was told many years ago about a body that kept reappearing. It wouldn't stay buried! The idea haunted me for decades. (Some stories hang in the back of your head for long periods, seemingly untended, patiently maturing in your subconscious as they wait for the optimum time to be written.) I tried out "Killing Charlie" on a live audience during two separate readings and garnered wild belly laughs on both occasions, and maybe you will also be amused. If so, I've done my job.

"Mama's Boy" is a story that highlights an ongoing threat in the movie world: the psychotic fan whose worship of a film icon spirals out of control.

Turning to verse, let me say that poetry has always occupied a very special place in my life. My poems have seen very limited distribution, and only a scant few Nolan readers are aware of the fact that—beyond my books, stories, and scripts—I have always written verse. My first creative effort, written at the age of nine, was a poem titled "The Fireman," which I scrawled in pencil in a lined, grade-school tablet.

A good poem represents the raw-boned distillation of thought and emotion. Each chosen word is vital if a poet is to achieve the ultimate in brevity and impact. At my average of two or three poems a year, I am not a prolific verse writer, yet each of my poems is deeply personal, an emotional escape valve, and an essential creative outlet from my innermost self.

"The Final Quest" can be credited to *Young Arthur*, an aborted television series I was once hired to write, about the early adventures of the legendary monarch. The poem emerged from my research for this ill-fated venture. Creative verse is a strange business, partaking of the mystical. This is certainly true of "The Final Quest," which seemed to write itself: the rhymed words spun out of my head as I recorded them on the page. It is a complex poem that—thanks to my subconscious mind—was actually quite easy for me to compose.

Three other poems ("American Journey," "Into Vienna," and "United Kingdom") have their basis in notes I recorded upon my return from cross-continental North American and European trips. I simply converted these notes into verse.

"Hemingway: Now Never There" was written after the famous author's death, and was originally printed as a cover poem in the elite pages of the literary magazine, *Prairie Schooner*. I later collected it as part of a limited-edition chapbook.

Several other poems also honor famous writers: radio's Norman Corwin in "Norman at Ninety"; Raymond Chandler in "Imagine Him"; Sylvia Plath in "Final Exit"; Dashiell Hammett in "After the Thin Man"; and Ray Bradbury in "God Bless!"

"The Horror Writer" was printed in a special "Nolan Issue" of *Weird Tales*, alongside a novella, an essay, a short story, and an interview. (As a reflection of my early days as a commercial artist, I also provided artwork for the issue.)

The book's title poem, "Have You Seen the Wind?," was composed as part of my only Western novel, *Rio Renegades*, and was written in tribute to my earliest role model: pulp king Max Brand (who always tried to include free verse in his Westerns).

"For My Wife" was written out of love and respect for my best friend, the finest person I've ever known, my writing companion and collaborator, Cameron Nolan. I met her when she was a teenager, and we've now been married for thirty-three years, with no end in sight. I cannot imagine life without Cam.

I won't go on, other than to say that each poem in this book is meaningful to me. The ones I have gathered here—both long and short—are my personal favorites.

I hope they find equal favor with you.

– William F. Nolan
West Hills, California

Stories

Behind the Curtain

Behind the Curtain

The city at night. Dark. Menacing. Dangerous. I've always equated a big city with a fatal disease: it can eat you alive. Muggings in dark alleys. Stoned teenage punks ready to cut your throat for the price of a fix. Serial killers on the prowl for fresh victims. I've never been mugged, or had my throat cut, or been stalked by a serial killer—but on one dark, rainswept Friday night the city finally nailed me.

I was driving home alone from a late movie at the local multiplex. I'm usually alone (divorced, no kids), so it was a normal night for me. The streets were slick from the storm, and my windshield wipers were barely able to keep up with the steady downrush of rain pelting the glass. Visibility was poor, so I didn't see the black Chevy Corvette until it hit me. Drunk driver. He'd run a red light and slammed broadside into my Mazda pickup. Twisted metal. Sirens. Cops.

The drunk went to jail and I woke up in the Manhattan Medical Center.

Which is where this bizarre story really begins…

I spent the first thirty-two hours after the accident in a coma. Everything was surreal. I'd sleep, have wild dreams I couldn't recall, then wake up to a nurse or a doctor probing me with needles or adjusting electronic sensors.

Finally, on the morning of the second day, I came out of it, clear-minded and wide awake. "How am I doing?" I asked the nurse, who had a plain honest face and very direct eyes.

"How do you *think* you're doing?" she countered.

Aside from a few large bruises and a bandaged cut on my forehead, I seemed to be unhurt. The Mazda's airbag had saved my life.

"I feel okay," I told the nurse. "No pain." I flexed my arms and legs. "No broken bones. So why am I still here?"

"You're under observation until the results of the final tests come in," she said. "You could still have internal injuries."

"But I feel all right," I said.

"The doctors have to make certain," she said. Her hospital name tag read ANNA. "Maybe you'll be able to leave later today," she added, as she took my temperature. "Your car is a total wreck. You're lucky to be alive."

I nodded.

"Just relax. Need anything, press the call button."

"Thanks, Anna," I said.

She exited through the hanging blue linen curtain that circled my bed.

"She's right, Buddy Boy. What that nurse said about you being lucky."

The voice came from a patient in the adjoining bed, who was hidden behind the blue curtain. A male voice. Probably late twenties, early thirties. But not happy. A sad voice.

"Me, I *never* been lucky," the man said. "All my life, I've never had no luck. The early days, when Ma left me on my uncle's farm, those days were okay. My Uncle Ned was real good to me. Treated me like a blood son. But I got itchy feet when I was sixteen. Lit out for the bright lights. Wanted to be a big city boy, and that's where all my bad luck started. Joined a street gang. Stole hubcaps and radios. Got in trouble with the law. I shoulda stayed on the farm with Uncle Ned."

"What about your mother? Didn't she—"

"Crap on my mother!" The voice was angry, laced with a cold hatred. "After she ditched me, dumped me on Uncle Ned, I never saw her again. She's probably dead by now. Who cares? She was a worthless bitch."

"And your father?"

"Never knew my old man. Ma said he was a bum with a hard-on. She met him in a bar. Ma drank like a fish."

"So what are you in here for?" I asked him.

"I got AIDS," he said. His voice took on a harder edge. "Can you frigging *believe* it? Me, Davey Leland, with AIDS!" A pause, then a deep sigh. "It all started when this big dude broke my jaw."

Obviously, he needed to talk, so I let him. Why not listen? I had nothing better to do and he had a lot to say.

"This guy was maybe six three," said the man behind the curtain. "Two hundred fifty pounds easy. Me, I'm just five eight. Hundred and thirty with rocks in my pocket. When he popped me, it was like getting hit by a concrete slab. Fractured my jaw. They had to wire my mouth shut. Ever try eating with your jaw wired? Everything I ate had to be put into a blender so I could suck it through a straw."

"What was the fight about?" I asked.

"I was working the ramp for Acorn Furniture," he said. "Helping unload stuff from the big rigs that rolled in. I was strong back then…strong for my size, anyway. Strong shoulders, strong arms. Not like I am now." I heard him sigh heavily. "Anyhow, this guy—name of Eddy Freez—he was the shift foreman and we didn't get along. Never liked me from the day I signed on. So he kept saying I wasn't working fast enough, that I was dogging it. And that made me sore, because the truth is, I was busting my butt on that ramp."

"And what he said to you—*that* started the fight?"

"Yeah, if you can call it a fight. I told Eddie he was full of shit, and bang! He popped me one on the jaw, and I went down like cut timber. Hit my head on the deck. Broke my jaw. And that was the start of the damn AIDS."

"What has a broken jaw to do with AIDS?" I asked.

"Well, first I got me a case of double pneumonia in the hospital, where they wired my jaw. Took me a while to get over the pneumonia. After I left, I looked up Eddy and hit him from behind with an iron pipe." He chuckled. "Gave him a nice concussion. Cops came along and threw me into the slammer. For aggravated assault."

"I see."

"Jail was a real bummer. I got raped by this other dude—in for armed robbery—and he gave me AIDS. See, the drugs they gave me for the lousy pneumonia had blown my immune system all to hell. Which is why I got the AIDS. Later, I started losing weight, and some bad-ass, freaky sores were spreading around my body, so I went to the hospital again and they said I had full-blown AIDS."

"Tough break," I said.

"It was my lousy luck," he said. "It's like all my life I been cursed. Once I got the bad word, I thought of offing myself, but I just didn't have the guts."

"Suicide isn't the answer," I said.

"Hell it isn't! Who's kidding who? I'm dying. Only thirty-four and I'm dying. Damnit, I'm still young!" His voice was strident. "I should have maybe forty or fifty years ahead of me. But not now. Not with AIDS. I'm on the road out."

"That's a pretty grim way to look at it," I said. "You should fight it. See yourself beating this thing."

"Easy for you to talk," he snapped back at me. "You bend up your car and walk out clean, while I *die* in here."

"I'm sorry," I said.

"Don't be. I don't need people being sorry for me." He stopped to cough. The sound was weak, like his body was all used up. "It wouldn't be that bad if it wasn't for Amy."

"Who's Amy?"

"My lady. We been together for a few years. When I got the news about the AIDS, I quit sleeping with her. The docs say you can use protection, but I didn't want to risk passing it on to her. So we just quit having sex."

"Did you tell her why?"

"No. Tried to, but I was chicken. Guess I was ashamed. When I stopped screwing her, she thought I didn't love her anymore. She took a powder. Left me flat." He coughed again. "I was wrong. I should of trusted Amy, told her the truth. She would of stuck with me. Letting her go was a big mistake."

"At least you see that now," I said.

"Hell, now I see a lot of things. When you're dying…it makes you think." He paused. "After Amy left, I got so weak I couldn't take care of myself any more. So here I am, in the frigging hospital, waiting to die."

"There's a lot of research being done on AIDS," I said. "Plenty of people working on it. They could find a cure any day." I spoke forcefully. "Use the power of your mind. Imagine all of your infected cells healing, one by one, and see the AIDS leaving your body. Miracles can happen."

"Not to *me* they can't," he shot back. "Not with my lousy luck."

Before I could say anything else the nurse came back, ducking through the blue curtain with a smile on her face.

"Good news," she said. "No internal problems." She handed me a release form signed by a doctor. "You can get dressed now; you're free to go. They'll check you out at the front desk and call you a cab so you can get home."

I thanked her, got out of bed, and put on my clothes. Then I decided to offer one last bit of encouragement to the poor guy in the next bed. Grasping the edge of the curtain, I pulled it aside.

The bed was empty. Mattress rolled up over the metal frame. No sheets or pillows.

"Nurse!" My voice was shaky.

Anna came through the curtain. "Yes?"

"I don't understand…in that bed…I was just talking to the man in that bed, but…he's gone. How could that be?"

"You've been in a bad accident," she told me. "It was traumatic, and your brain may take a while to completely clear. Hearing voices is not uncommon in your situation."

"But this was *real*," I protested. "The *man* was real. He told me his name was Davey."

Anna frowned. "That's odd," she said. "There *was* a patient in that bed named David, but he died a week ago…"

I stared at her.

"…of AIDS."

The Ex

The Ex

It was late afternoon on a weekday. Clear and sunny. Not a cloud in the sky. Perfect baseball weather. When the door chimed I walked from the den to answer it. No servants. Not since the divorce. So it took me a while to reach the front door. The chime was kicking echoes off the hallway when I got there. Whoever it was lacked patience.

I peered through the barred square in the door's center panel. Two young men in neat gray suits. Red ties. Neat and smiling, both of them. One tall, one short. The short one was carrying a leather case. "Who is it?" I asked.

"We'd like to talk to you, sir," the tall one said.

The short one unzipped the case and took out a baseball bat. He waved it in the air, still smiling. Nice teeth.

"I don't sign those anymore," I said. "No gloves or balls either. Sorry."

The short one nodded. "That's okay, sir. It's a real privilege, just being able to meet you in person. My son Bobby, he's seven. Thinks you're great. Rates you just below Spider Man."

I grinned. Kid must be a big fan.

"Is it possible we could talk to you, sir?" asked the tall one. "I mean, just for a few minutes maybe?"

"Be a real honor," said the short one.

I shrugged. Well, why not? I'd been dealing with ball fans for most of my adult life. In fact, now that I was retired, things were a little empty. I missed the ego-boost that fans can provide. Hell, I might even sign their damned bat!

17

"Step inside," I said, unlatching the door and swinging it back. "You fellas ever watch me play?"

"Me, I did!" said the tall one. He had a high, girlish voice, sandy hair, and a bland, unremarkable face. "I saw you homer in the ninth, with the bases loaded, in that last World Series game. Boy, you really smacked the old apple! The crowd went apeshit."

I nodded, leading them into the den, chuckling at the memory. "Yeah, that was one of my better days. After we won the Series I decided to hang it up, leave on a high note. I'm just too frigging old to compete with all the young Turks. Man has to know when to quit. I've seen ballplayers go on for years past their prime and I've watched them lose the magic. It's a damn sad sight. When the magic's gone you've hit bottom. I quit while my name still meant something."

"Well, it sure means a lot in our family," said the short man. "My Dad, he used to talk to me about Babe Ruth all the time—the same way I talk to Bobby about you."

I was flattered. "Want me to sign that bat?"

The little guy was amazed. He had a round, pumpkin face, and now it lit up. "But I thought you didn't–"

"I'll make an exception," I said as he removed the bat from its case. Handed it over. I hefted it, swung it lightly. "Nice balance."

"Made the case for it myself," he said. "Custom leather. Special grain. Wanted to be sure it was protected."

I looked more closely. Pro model 125, an H&B Louisville Slugger 35-incher. Nice.

"DiMaggio used a Slugger," the little man said. "Early in his career. A model D 29. Me, I used to have a Spalding, but it cracked. They don't make 'em anymore."

"Not since the Second World War," I said, signing the H&B with a felt tip and handing it back to him.

"Hey—I'm really very appreciative," he said. "You know, my sister-in-law *hates* baseball! Can you imagine anyone hating baseball?"

"To each his own," I said.

"I just can't figure it," the little man continued. "Women! You can never figure a woman." He snorted. "Alma—that's her name—she thinks baseball is stupid. Makes no sense to her, all these guys running around these bases. I took Alma to just *one* ball game. She liked the open stadium, and the clipped green grass on the field, and the smells of hot popcorn and peanuts—but when the game started she was bored silly. Dozed through most of it. Women! You can never figure a woman. Sometimes, I think they live in a different universe!"

The tall one had been admiring my trophy case. "Must give you a great deal of satisfaction, having earned these."

I nodded. "At least they prove I was out there. Sometimes, my whole career seems unreal, as if it all happened in a dream." I shrugged. "But I guess a lot of retired players feel that way."

"Yeah, I remember your saying that—about it all being like a dream—in the *Sports Illustrated* interview," said the short man. "The one with your picture on the cover."

"I was pissed about that interview. Copy editor cut it in half when they printed it. Made me sound like an idiot. The transcript I saw of the original was twice that length. But then again, my wife was always telling me that I talk too much."

The tall guy turned away from the trophy case to face me. His smile had faded, and he had a hard, intense look. "We didn't come here to get the bat signed."

"Oh." I met his steady gaze. "Then why did you come here?"

"Because of her," he said.

"Her?"

"You know," added the little guy. "Your ex."

I stared at them. "Are you saying that my *wife* sent you?"

"In a manner of speaking," said the tall one.

"But she's dead!"

"We know," said the short one. "That's why we're here."

"I don't understand."

"She wanted it this way," the tall guy told me. "Set it up before she died. Made all the arrangements personally. She seemed to get a kick out of it. Sort of chortled when she laid out what we were to do." He gave me a long stare. "Guess she didn't like you much."

"She *hated* me," I said. "Only stayed with me because of the money I was making—and because of who I was. She enjoyed being hooked to a celebrity…being identified as my wife. It made her feel important, since she had no talent of her own."

"Why did you put up with it?" This from the short guy.

"Because a divorce is costly, and I knew she'd blame the failure of our marriage on me. And I was right. She did. Hired a Beverly Hills lawyer. Jeez, but I got burned by that bitch. I knew she hated me—but until the divorce I didn't know how deep her hatred was."

"Yeah," piped the small guy, "you wouldn't have liked what she said about you. Not very complimentary."

In thinking about my ex, I'd lost focus on just why the two of them were here. They still hadn't told me. I was suddenly angry. They were working for the bitch! Even beyond her death, she was still hounding me.

"If you've come for money—"

"No, we're being well paid," said the tall man. "Money isn't what this is about."

"Then, damn you, man! Why *are* you here?"

"To execute her orders," said the short guy. "To do our job."

I was distinctly uneasy. Whatever my ex had in mind would be negative. Something dark. Maybe even...I backed away toward the desk. "She sent you here to kill me!"

They both chuckled, shaking their heads.

"Naw," said the tall man. "Killing's not our line. The company has people who do that. Special people. But that's not us."

"Then I don't understand why you—"

"Back up a minute," said the tall guy. "Let's not rush. We're enjoying ourselves here."

"That's right," said the short one. "This is very enjoyable."

"You still watch the games?" the tall one asked.

"Uh...yes, of course. Just because I don't play anymore doesn't mean that I—"

"Bet you've got yourself a swell TV setup," said the short man. "I mean, big screen, Dolby sound...the works."

"It's adequate," I said.

"And that red silk robe you're wearing," said the tall one. "Must of cost plenty. The wife, she loves red silk. She'd look real snappy in a robe like you're wearing."

Despite my basic apprehension, they were making me angry. "Quit stalling," I snapped. "My ex had a purpose in sending you here. I want to know what's going on."

"In due time," said the tall man, grinning at me. "We've got all day."

"Yeah," said the other. "Our schedule is very loose." He took up a hitter's stance in the middle of the room, legs spaced, bat to shoulder. "When I was a kid I dreamed of playing in the major leagues," he said. "I was pretty good, too. I could sock the old apple pretty good." He swung at an invisible ball. "But I was too short to make the school team, let alone any pro team. Just too runty, they said. God, but I hate being called a runt." He looked at me. "At least you're tall, like my buddy here. Tall guys they never call runts."

"The irony is, he gets to work with a bat after all," said the tall guy in his musical voice. "He's our official batboy."

The little guy grunted. "Not much like playing in the majors, but it's a living."

"Shall we tell him exactly what we're here for?" the tall one asked the runt.

"Yeah, let's tell him."

"It's like this," explained the tall one. "Because you're kind of an icon to our kids, and because we both respect you personally, we're gonna give you a choice."

The runt hefted his bat. "Just one good smash. Kneecap or elbow. Your choice."

"Christ!" I breathed. "You mean to cripple me!"

"Not really," said the tall man. "You'll get over it. I'm sure you've got a real good doc. He can set the bone, maybe replace the parts that are too smashed up."

"You'll be fine," said the runt.

"How much are you getting paid for this?" I asked them. "I'll *triple* your rate!"

"That's bribery," said the runt, shaking his head. "We can't be bribed. We're pros. We've got our pride. Doing a job like this, it's not as simple as it sounds. You have to know just where to hit, and exactly how hard. Requires a lot of time to master the craft. I take pride in what I do. Money can't buy pride."

The tall guy put his hand on my shoulder. "The good thing about this is that your ex didn't die while you were still a player. This would have ruined you for the game."

"He's right," said the short one. "I'm just glad we didn't have to do this earlier. Now it's okay, with you being retired and all. It won't be a big problem for you."

The runt walked closer to me, idly swinging the bat.

"I'd advise you to choose the right elbow, since you're a southpaw. Then you can still use the other arm."

"Yeah," nodded the tall guy. "Kneecap's a bitch to heal. The bones don't knit as well, and you spend a long time on crutches. More pain there, too. I'd definitely go for the elbow. But…" He shrugged. "It's your choice."

"I'll phone the police," I said tightly. "They'll deal with this."

"Stay away from the police," the runt warned me, eyes flashing. "You try to call in Johnny Law and I'll *really* smash you. I mean, a bad scene for you. By the time the cops get here you'll be a bloody mess. Heck, I don't want to have to do that to you. *Especially* not to you—being a personal hero of mine."

"You bastards!"

They both smiled blandly. "You don't have to like us for doing our job," said the tall man, "but we're not vindictive like your ex. She was definitely vindictive."

"Definitely," said the runt. "She arranged all this so you'd have, to quote the lady, 'something to remember her by.' Unquote."

"Damn her!" I snapped. "Damn her lousy soul!"

"Well, let's get to it," said the tall one.

"You name it, sir," said the runt. "Kneecap or elbow. Left or right side."

I realized that I had absolutely no option. I couldn't call the police. I couldn't escape. There was no one else in the house to help me. So I made my choice.

"Left kneecap," I said softly. "I need to use both arms. For the keyboard." I flushed. "I'm writing a book about my career."

"Okay, then," said the tall man, walking quickly behind me and pinning my shoulders in a wrestler's hold. "Go ahead. Go for the leg."

The runt took his hitting stance, looking serious. The bat was on his shoulder.

"Play ball!" piped the tall guy.

The runt smashed me.

The pain was incredible.

When the tall guy let go of me I collapsed to the den floor, screaming through clenched teeth. I was gripping my smashed knee, in agony. I'd been hurt plenty of times on the field, but it was nothing compared to this.

"You should have gone for an elbow shot," said the runt. "Kneecap's always worse." He carefully replaced the bat in its custom leather zipcase. "Well," he said to his partner. "Game's over."

The tall one leaned down, his face close to mine. "If you try to do anything about this, like calling in the police or anything, the company will send some other people over here to kill you. And I know you don't want that to happen."

"Right," nodded the runt. "Life is precious. Nobody wants to die."

All this happened five years ago.

I've walked crookedly ever since.

Listening to Billy

Listening to Billy

After he'd killed her, Arthur decided he would cut his throat, but he had plenty of time for that. There was no hurry. First, the roses in the back yard needed watering, so that's what he did next. He watered the roses, making sure the hose pressure wasn't too strong. You can damage roses if you use too much hose pressure. He was wearing only his blue-striped boxer shorts and a pajama top, but no one noticed him out there in the back yard, watering his roses.

After he'd finished, he turned off the hose and coiled it neatly, putting it back on its proper hook in the garage. Everything in the garage was clean and orderly. Arthur Joergens was a very orderly man. All of the tools were in their proper places and the 1954 family Chevrolet (only a year old!) was under a dust cover. Even in a closed garage, he knew, dust can eat into body paint. He didn't drive the Chevrolet much anymore, now that he'd turned sixty. I guess sixty isn't that old, he told himself, but he just didn't feel that he had the reflexes of a young man anymore when it came to driving in heavy traffic.

And, of course, Adele never drove the Chevrolet. She kept telling him that she was a licensed, fully capable driver. She thought his strict prohibition against her driving was ridiculous, but he didn't trust a woman behind the wheel. When they bought the Chevy he told her he would do all the driving. Later, after they'd had the car for a couple of months, he thought about letting her drive. She smiled (sweet smile) and said that would be nice, but nothing came of it. Last Thanksgiving, when he turned sixty, he thought maybe he should let her drive the next time they went to the lake house, but when they got there, he changed his mind.

However, the matter of her driving or not driving was now settled. With Adele lying in the kitchen, those two bullets in her head, she definitely wouldn't be driving the Chevrolet to the lake house.

The lake house.

The lake house.

Back in the kitchen, the words were constant drumbeats inside his head as he washed blood from his hands at the sink. The lake house had been the reason he'd killed Adele. That, and what Billy told him in the tavern.

"Kill her, Art. It's the only thing makes any sense. Ya really hafta kill her."

The first time he'd gone into the tavern to have a cold beer in the afternoon—to get out of Missouri's summer sun, which can boil a man's brains—Billy had taken the stool next to him at the bar. Back in the 1800s, Kansas City had been the starting point of the old Santa Fe Trail, and—in keeping with the city's history—the tavern had been decked out in Old West décor. The walls were filled with faded sepia photographs of old-timers and wagon trains on their way to California and other points west. Billy fit right in, dressed like he was, Western style.

"I'm Billy," he said. "What's yer handle?"

"I'm Arthur Joergens."

"Howdy, Art!" They shook hands. Billy's grip was soft, like a young girl's. A soft handshake.

"So…whatcha do fer a livin', Art?"

"I put in concrete basements," he told Billy. "I pour the concrete, cover the dirt floor and walls with it, smooth it out and they pay me for that."

"You married, Art?"

"Yes, I am. To a fine woman. Adele. Met her at a church picnic. She let me take her home on the back of my motorcycle. Of course, that was when I still had one. I don't own a cycle anymore."

"Me, I ride a horse," said Billy. "You can always depend on a horse. A horse can be a real friend."

"I suppose that's true," said Arthur. "I've no direct experience with horses."

"My Daddy had me on the back of a horse practical a'fore I could walk," said Billy. "Me and horses, we get along."

"I'm sure you do," said Arthur.

"This woman a'yours…ya really love her, right?"

"Yes, I do. Indeed I do. Adele is a perfect wife. She respects me. Knows her place. I'm the boss. I make all the decisions."

Billy narrowed his eyes. They were narrow to begin with. Kind of squinty. "You *trust* her, Art?"

"Absolutely," said Arthur Joergens. "I trust Adele absolutely one hundred percent."

"Well, ya better watch out for her," Billy had told him on that first afternoon. "You can trust a horse, but you can't trust a woman."

Arthur sipped his cold beer. When he looked back at the bar stool next to him, it was empty.

A week later, after watching Adele very closely, Arthur was back in the tavern.

Billy was on the next stool, wearing a plaid shirt (out at one elbow), and scuffed leather chaps, with a heavy Colt jammed into his belt. He took off his battered sombrero and ran a hand along the sweat-stained brim.

"Gotta get me a new hat," he said. "This one's all wore to hell."

"It's very weathered," said Arthur.

"Yeah," nodded Billy, staring down at the hat. "Weathered is what it is." He placed the sombrero on the bar.

"Do you still ride a horse?" Arthur asked.

"Yep," nodded Billy. "Always have. Always will."

"Does your horse have a name?"

"Nope." Billy shrugged. "I just call him horse. Whoa, horse. Giddyup, horse." He snickered. It was not a pleasant sound.

"Where do you keep the animal?"

"Out back." Billy jerked a thumb toward the rear of the tavern. "Got him hitched out back."

Arthur noticed that Billy's nails were ragged and encrusted with dirt. He wondered when Billy had last taken a shower. His hair was thick with grease and looked matted. Hadn't been combed in a long time. Arthur prided himself on his personal hygiene, and was quick to note the lack of it in others.

"May I ask why you wear a gun?"

"Protection," said Billy. "Lotta folks want my hide. Hafta defend myself. Galoot comes in, all hot an' bothered, lookin' to get a rep for killin' me, I hafta kill him first."

"Have you killed many people?"

"Sure have," said Billy. "One fer each year'a my life. I'm twenty-one, an' I've killed me twenty-one."

"That's a lot of killing."

"Yep, but it's like I said, I hafta defend myself." He patted the Colt's worn handle. "Old Judge Colt here does the job."

"Any regrets?"

"About what?"

"About shooting twenty-one people."

"Naw. They had it comin' ever'time." He put one of his soft hands on Arthur's shoulder. "Look, Art, shootin' somebody is no big deal. Let's suppose you shot Adele. That would be no big deal."

"Oh, Lordy, I'd never do a thing like that," declared Arthur. He smiled, shaking his head at the thought.

"Got an iron to home?"

"An iron?" Arthur looked confused. "Adele has one. She irons all my clothes."

"Naw. I mean a shootin' iron. A gun. You got a gun?"

"Well...yes. My grandfather was a police officer in Chicago at the turn of the century. Played the stock market on the side. He invested unwisely, and died penniless. All he left behind was his old service revolver, which I inherited. I keep it in the roll-top desk in the den."

"Still work?"

"I suppose it still works," nodded Arthur. "Of course, I've never fired it. I've taken it apart from time to time to clean it."

"Good fer you!" said Billy. "Me, I do the same for this here one." He took out his Colt and flourished it. Arthur noticed that the gun seemed to have been well cared for.

"Got bullets?"

Arthur nodded. "Yes, I have a box of rounds in the same top drawer. I assume they're for grandfather's weapon, but I've never attempted to insert them in the chamber."

"Gun's no good without bullets—just like your pecker," Billy said, snickering again. He took his sombrero from the bar, whacked it against his chaps to knock off some dust, then put the hat back on. The brim flopped loosely, giving him a lopsided look. "You been watchin' Adele?"

Arthur was embarrassed to admit that he had.

"She been spendin' yer money?"

"Well…she buys things, of course. Adele sure does like gloves."

"How many she got?"

"I've never counted."

"Got a dozen pair maybe?"

"Yes, easily that. I'd say more."

"Wastin' yer money, Art. Nobody needs all them gloves."

"Adele thinks otherwise," Arthur stated. "She has different colors to go with different outfits. Several pairs of white, because she says that no matter what a woman does, white gloves get dirty and must be changed. That's why, when she's wearing white, she always has a spare pair or two along in her purse. In case they get dirty and have to be changed while she's out. Then she says she needs at least two pairs each of black and gray, plus a pair of navy blue to match her good coat, and a special, long pair to wear to weddings and such. And last winter she bought a pair of red gloves, just because she liked the color. Said wearing them made her hands feel warmer when it was freezing outside."

"That's a lotta crap, if you ask me," said Billy. "Ya gotta put yer foot down, Art. Tell her flat—no more damn gloves."

"But I can't—"

"No buts about it," declared Billy. "Tell her flat."

Arthur frowned. "I think you're right. I'll tell her."

"You do that, Art. An' keep a sharp eye on her. Remember, ya can't ever trust a woman."

Then he was gone.

Two weeks later Arthur was back in the tavern. Tired and sweaty. He'd just put in a concrete basement over on Paseo for a woman who couldn't speak English. Big Italian woman who shouted constantly, thinking that if she just kept yelling, Arthur would understand what she was saying. He needed a cold beer.

The tavern was deserted when he'd walked in. Arthur sat down on his favorite stool at the bar, alone. When his beer arrived, and he turned to pay the bartender, there was Billy, perched on the next stool. He looked dusty.

"Hiya, Art."

"Hello, Billy." Arthur didn't know the youth's last name, and never asked. None of his business.

"You look kinda bushed," said Billy.

"I am. Exhausted, really. Pouring concrete is rough work. Maybe I'm getting too old for the job."

"How's the wife?"

"We had a bad argument last night. She wasn't speaking to me when I left the house this morning."

"Whatcha argue about?"

"I did as you said," Arthur told him. "I put my foot down about the gloves. She bought another pair last week—said she needed them to match her favorite summer dress—and so I said no more. No more damn gloves."

"That's the stuff!" Billy grinned at him. A stupid grin. Arthur had to admit that Billy actually looked retarded, but what the young man said seemed logical.

"She blew up," Arthur related. "Told me I had no right on God's green earth to dictate how many gloves she could buy. Said she got the new pair on sale, and she had a right to something special for herself if she used money she'd saved from her food budget. I told her the food budget was for *food*, and if she had enough money left over to buy gloves from it, then I needed to cut her allowance because I was obviously giving her too much. We had a bad argument."

"Bet ya felt like killin' her, right?"

"Oh, no," said Arthur, shocked at the idea. "Nothing that severe. I admit that I was very angry at her, but I guess all married couples have their squabbles. It was just a family squabble."

"Ya have many?"

"Never used to," said Arthur. "Now we seem to fight quite a lot. Just lately." He sighed. "We've been fighting a lot lately."

"Mind if I ask a real personal question?"

"No, go right ahead."

"What in tarnation keeps ya together?"

"I don't follow you."

"What's the glue that keeps you an' her stuck together?"

"Uh, well…" Arthur hesitated. "Adele has always been very loving toward me. Very considerate of my feelings. At least that's the way she used to be. But…things have changed. Don't know why, but they have."

"Got any kids?"

"No." Arthur shook his head. "No children. Always been painful to me, not being a father. I was raised in a big house full of brothers and sisters. I wanted children, but Adele didn't. She grew up an only child. Thinks children are messy, that they can't be properly controlled. Always underfoot. Better not to have them. Know what she used to say?"

"Tell me," said Billy.

"Adele used to say there are enough children in this world without us adding to the number. Not up to us to help populate the human race."

Billy grunted, saying nothing.

"Adele was quite firm in her viewpoint—how she felt about not having children. I went along with her. I didn't pursue the matter."

"So I guess you're not the boss after all," said Billy. "It's Adele who really calls the shots."

"I've never thought about it that way," said Arthur.

"She's a sly one," declared Billy. "Usin' you like a puppet. Adele pulls the strings, an' you jump."

"Oh, no, that's not the case," said Arthur. "Adele abides by my decisions."

"Sure—long as they fit what *she* wants to do." Billy spat on the tavern floor. Ugly habit. "You own any property, Art?"

"Why, yes, we do," nodded Arthur. It was cool in the tavern, in contrast to the day's searing heat, but Arthur tugged at his shirt collar. His clothes felt restricting, tight against his skin. "We own our house on Harrison," he told the youth. "Two bedrooms, with a den. I put in the basement myself. And we're buying a small summer place at the lake."

"What lake would that be?"

"Tapawingo," said Arthur. "We go there in August, when it gets really hot and humid in the city."

"Yeah, gets dang hot in New Mexico, too."

"I take a couple of weeks off each August and we drive out to the lake. To Tapawingo."

"Like to fish, Art?"

"Yes, I do, and I'm a fair hand at catching trout. My father used to take me to the Lake of the Ozarks. He taught me how to fly cast. We were very close. Died of cancer."

"I did me some fishin' once," said Billy. "Kinda bored me, tellya the truth. Me, I like *action*, an' ya don't get much out of fishin'."

"Well... to each his own," said Arthur.

A silence between them as Arthur Joergens sipped his beer.

"Want me to put a head on that?" asked the bartender.

"No, no. I'm fine," said Arthur.

"Ya believe in ghosts?" asked Billy.

"I suppose they *could* exist," said Arthur. "Never thought much about them, one way or the other."

"Me, I believe in 'em," declared the youth. "But not ever'body who kicks off becomes one. Just them with a job to do back in life."

"That's an interesting theory," said Arthur.

"Yeah," nodded Billy. "I sure as heck believe in ghosts."

Again, the conversation trailed off into silence. Finally, Arthur spoke in a low monotone.

"Adele thinks I'm spending too much on the lake house. Had to put on a new roof last year because of winter snow damage. Then the boat's engine went on the fritz and I had to buy another. An engine, that is. Plus new lumber to fix our dock. The boards were rotting. Since I'm a basement contractor, I got the lumber at discount, but it still cost a lot more than I expected. The rock chimney needs repair, too. Adele says she's having trouble with the wood cookstove in the kitchen, and next year the county's going to force us to put in a cesspool. They say the lake is being poisoned by outhouse seepage. The house is beautiful, but it was built back before the turn of the century. It's starting to fall apart, and that's a fact."

"Place means a lot to ya, huh?"

"Yes, it's my only refuge." Arthur smiled at the phrase. "I mean, I look forward to going there all year long. Just thinking about those two weeks in August makes me feel good. Nights at the lake are really peaceful, with the water lying all quiet under the moon. The air's so clear you can see every star. I really *relax* at the lake."

"But Adele, she resents it, huh?"

"I wouldn't go that far. She just thinks it costs too much, keeping it up properly, making the payments, and all."

Billy shook his head. "Adele don't want ya to have the lake house, Art. Plain as shit on a stick. She'll find a way to make ya give it up."

"That's simply not true," Arthur countered. "Adele enjoys herself out at the lake."

"Ever say so?"

"Say *what*?"

"That she enjoys bein' there."

"Well...not exactly. Not in so many words, but I can tell she likes it."

"Yer kiddin' yerself, pardner," said Billy. "She hates it."

That August, at the lake house, Arthur asked Adele if she was happy being there.

"Happy?" Her eyes were vague. "I suppose so."

They were sitting out on the porch, facing the water. The sun was setting and a motorboat, far out on the lake, made a tiny insect buzz. To Arthur, it was a comforting sound.

"You don't *seem* happy," he said.

"Well, I have a lot of things to do back home," Adele said.

"This *is* our home. For the next two weeks it is."

"Not our *real* home," she said.

"It's real to me," he told her.

"You like to fish and swim," said Adele, "and I don't. So I just sit around here, waiting for you with nothing to do."

"Can't you just enjoy the beauty?" Arthur asked. "It's like a little piece of paradise out here."

"What's so wrong with Kansas City?"

"It's hot and muggy and jammed with people," Arthur said vehemently.

"There's nothing to do out here," she said.

"You used to make butterscotch ice cream," Arthur reminded her. "When we first came here, you made wonderful butterscotch ice cream."

"Uh-huh," she said listlessly.

"Why did you stop?"

"Too fattening," she said. "I have to watch my weight."

"I *loved* eating your butterscotch ice cream," said Arthur.

"Uh-huh," said Adele.

When Arthur told Billy about the ice cream the youth slapped his battered sombrero against the bar. "What'd I tell ya!" he declared. "She resents yer having the lake house. She won't even make you ice cream, even when she admits she doesn't have anything better to do."

"Adele keeps talking about how high the mortgage payments are," Arthur said, staring into his beer. "Last week, after we returned from Tapawingo, she said we should think about selling the place. Let somebody else worry about paying off the mortgage."

"There ya are," nodded Billy. "Tryin' to take away the one thing that means somethin' special to you. Oh, sure, it's just dandy her buyin' all them gloves she don't need, but when it comes ta what *you* want…" He let his voice trail off.

"I told her, damnit, I'd never sell the place," declared Arthur. "That there was no room for discussion."

"But ya argued about it, right?"

Arthur nodded wearily. "Yes. Another bad argument. Adele said some nasty things."

"Kill her, Art," said Billy. "It's the only thing makes any sense. Ya really hafta kill her."

"I could never do a thing like that," Arthur declared.

"Hey, it's real easy," said Billy, pulling the heavy Colt from his belt. He aimed it at the bartender. "Bang!" he said. Then he gave Arthur another stupid grin. "Easy."

That was a week ago. Early this morning, they had another bad argument. In the kitchen. Arthur and Adele kept the front rooms for holidays like Christmas and Easter, when relatives came by. The rest of the year they lived in the back of the house: kitchen, bedroom, bathroom, and den. Arthur kept his collection of antique clocks in the basement. (Adele claimed that all the ticking kept her awake at night, but she never chided him about the cost of the clocks, and he appreciated that.)

She was adamant, though, about the lake house. Adele told Arthur he would have to sell it because—now that he was sixty, and his concrete basement business was slowing down—they couldn't afford such a major expense anymore. Either he sold the house, or she would leave him. Simple as that. No more mortgage payments.

He yelled at her. She yelled back at him. Then Arthur walked into the den, to the roll-top desk, opened the top drawer, took out his grandfather's gun, loaded it from the box of bullets, walked back to the kitchen, and shot Adele twice in the head.

When he got to the tavern that afternoon, after deciding not to cut his throat until he'd talked to Billy, he found the place deserted. Just him and the bartender, whose name was Jake. Big man, tall and beefy, with a front tooth missing.

"Where's Billy?" asked Arthur.

"Billy who?"

"The young kid I talk to all the time when I come in here," Arthur said peevishly. "The one in the sombrero."

"I never saw you talk to nobody," said the bartender. "You always come in alone, drink a beer or two, argue with yourself, mutter a lot of stuff about your wife—and then you leave. Period."

"What?" Arthur drew in a sharp breath. "Are you *blind*? Billy comes in here all the time. We have good talks. He understands my problems. With my wife, Adele. The problems I have with her." His voice became heated. "Billy really *understands*. He's the only one who does. He really understands."

"Look, mister," said the bartender in a patient tone, "it's like I said. You been in here alone every damn time."

"Told me he was twenty-one," murmured Arthur. "Has an old gun in his belt. Wears a dirty sombrero. Keeps his horse out back."

"*Horse?*" snorted Jake. "Nobody around here rides a horse. Maybe all them beers have gone to your head."

Arthur suddenly pressed forward against the bar, pointing. "That's him. In the photo. That's him!"

It was Billy all right. With the brim of his hat all loose and lopsided. And with those squinty eyes and that stupid grin on his face.

The barman swung around to look at the back wall of the tavern. At a framed portrait which hung next to a big photograph of a Santa Fe Trail wagon train.

The big man smiled broadly. "You really had me goin' there for a minute," he said. "Fella in that picture hasn't been talking to you or anybody else for a mighty long time. Not since he was shot by Pat Garrett back in 1881. That's Billy the Kid."

Arthur Joergens didn't move. He continued to stare at the framed photo of the young outlaw.

"You want a beer?" asked the bartender.

In Real Life

In Real Life

She came into the room raving as usual in that shrill voice of hers. Like a train whistle. Or nails on a blackboard. Called me a fucking loser. Said I wasn't worth cat shit. Raved and shouted, waving her hands around. Swearing like a mill hand. Eyes blazing at me, like two hot coals.

She made it easy, killing her. Like the end of that Mickey Spillane book where Mike Hammer shoots the evil bitch in the belly. I just walked into the bedroom and took the gun from her vanity table where she always kept it for protection. Paranoid. Afraid of intruders, of being raped. As if anyone would want to.

What are you doing with my gun? she yells. Always yelling. Mouth like an open sewer. I said I took the gun to shut her up for good. You're gonna kill me? She laughed her hyena laugh. Real unattractive. You couldn't kill a fucking fly, she tells me. Oh, no, that's not true…I can kill you okay, I said. No problem. My voice was icy calm. This was the Big Moment.

That's when I fired point-blank at her: Bang, bang, bang.

She flopped over like a big rag doll. Kind of comical. But she really messed up the sofa, falling across it with all that blood coming out of her. Ruined it, really. You can't ever get blood out of a white sofa. That was when Bernie said, in his quiet way: cut and print.

How was I? Linda asked him. Did I fall the right way? You were perfect, darling, he told her. They hugged. Directors always hug their female stars. Treat them like children. That's because every actress is insecure. They need a lot of attention. Best I get is a pat on the shoulder. Good job, Chuck.

He held that gun too close to me, Linda complained. The wads from those fucking blanks *hurt* me.

41

Linda was like the bitch in the movie. She liked to say fuck. Tough broad. One of the boys. Never liked her. Third picture with her and we still didn't get along. Strong mutual dislike from the first day we met. None of the crew liked her either. Always complaining. Didn't approve of the way her hair was fixed: too short on the sides, too rigid on top. The pale make-up made her look like a corpse. Her dress didn't do her figure justice. The sound man was an asshole, didn't maintain her modulation level. The head grip smoked too much on his breaks. His clothes reeked of stale cigar smoke. Always something to criticize.

But she saved her prime complaints for me. I blocked her key light. Stepped on her lines. Hogged the camera. Wouldn't stick to the script. (She hated improv because she couldn't handle it herself. No flexibility.)

Killing her had been a pleasure. Wouldn't mind doing it in real life. Not that I would. I'm no psycho. Don't go around killing foul-mouthed fe-males. But getting paid for faking it was satisfying. I got to kill Linda in two of our pics together. Strangled her in *The Dark Stranger* and stuck her in a food freezer in *Wake Up to Death*. Fun. A flat-out pleasure.

Ralph handed the pages back to me. "I don't believe it," he said, a nasty edge to his voice.

"Why not?" I demanded. "What's wrong with it?"

"Everything," said Ralph. He seemed to take special delight in hurting me. "You just don't know how to get into the male mind. It takes a man to write about another man."

"That's crap and you know it," I snapped back at him. "Women have been writing successfully about men for three thousand years."

"Okay." Ralph shrugged his scarecrow shoulders. "Maybe they have—but these pages fail to convince me that you're one of them."

"This is my fifth novel for Christ's sake," I protested. "If I'm so lousy, then how come Viking keeps buying them?"

"Hey, Linda! Get real. Your other books all had female protagonists." Ralph had that know-it-all grin on his face. "You wrote them from a femi-nine perspective. A man is different. It's obvious that you can't handle the male viewpoint."

"That's your opinion," I said. "I know exactly what I'm doing. *I'm* the writer, chum."

"And I'm your best editor!"

"Yeah, and my *worst* husband."

"Then why did you marry me?"

"Damned if I know. Guess I figured you'd be a step up from my first three. But I was wrong. You're a step *down*."

"You're a stupid cunt."

"And you're a stupid prick."

I looked him straight in the eye. "I want a divorce," I said.

And that's when I killed her.

Killed the character in my novel, I mean. This is as far as I got. Thing just wasn't working for me. No flow. Jagged. I was forcing it. And it wasn't truthful. For example, women can write beautifully about men, they do it all the time. Look at Joyce Carol Oates. She writes men that breathe on the page. Eudora Welty. Shirley Jackson. And lots of others.

So that part was all wrong. Yet if I had Linda's husband *approve* of her scenes then my structural conflict would be missing. I could do it over, but I just lost heart. And this novel-within-a-novel stuff is tricky to bring off.

There was something else. Using my dead wife's name for the female character was a bad idea. I should have called her something else. Any name but Linda.

Maybe I'm not cut out to be a novelist. Maybe I should just stick to directing other people's scripts. That's what I'm really good at. Hell, in France they think I'm another Jerry Lewis. Not that I do comedy; I don't. But the Frenchies love me. Edgar Price is a genius. That's what they say. In Frogland, I'm a hot property.

Writing about my dead wife was painful. Bitter memories. Linda drove me nuts during our marriage. We were never compatible. People still believe she died of "natural causes," I made sure about that. Used a poison you can't trace. My little secret. Her family was convinced of my grief. Kept my head lowered at the funeral, dabbing at my eyes. In the cemetary I leaned down to plant a kiss on her coffin. And the single rose I tossed into the grave was a lovely touch.

Guess I shouldn't be admitting it all here, in this diary. But no one will read it. Who'd ever think of looking for a floor safe in a garden shed? Ideal hiding place. That's where the diary goes each morning before I leave for the studio. And I keep the safe's combination inside my head. Never wrote it down. I'm no fool.

Well, at least Linda's gone. I'm damn well rid of her. No more arguments about money, or my drinking, or my women. That loud mouth of hers is shut forever. Comforting thought.

Oops, a horn outside. The limo is here, so I've got to wind this up. End of entry.

Off to the daily grind.

Killing him was easy. Big shot director. Big *shit* is more like it. With all his fancy clothes, and his foreign cars, and his big house in Bel Air. Claims he saved my ass. Said I'd be nothing if he hadn't come along. Probably be waiting tables at Denny's. Bull! I've always had talent, even as a little girl in Kansas City. Mama used to brag about me to all the neighbors. I'd do those little skits of mine, dancing and singing, and Mama would clap like crazy and tell me I was another Judy Garland. (But I could always dance better than Judy Garland.)

Edgar Price, the big shot director. Discovered me, he always said. Well, *someone* would have. He just happened to get a hard-on in that dumb little theatre play in Pasadena when I showed a lot of leg. Came backstage after the curtain to tell me that I demonstrated "genuine talent" and that the studio was looking for talent like mine. Yeah, sure. *He* was the one looking—at my tits, not my talent.

He did get me into pictures, if you can call the kind of crap he directed a picture. Cheezy horror stuff, with me playing a nude corpse in the first one. Not a frigging line in the whole movie. *The Blood Queen's Revenge*. Yuck.

Then he had me doing bare-ass scenes in a shower for that crappy film of his about women in the Air Force. I was supposed to be a lesbian jet pilot. A nothing part. I had maybe five minutes of screen time and I was butt-naked for most of that.

Next, he put me in his wrestling thing, where I was this female wrestler who gets her clothes torn off in the ring. Just the pits.

And then was the one where I played a doomed prostitute with lung cancer. God! How I hated the scene where I died in the bathtub. They got worried when my nipples stayed erect, which they said should not happen when I was dead. But that bathwater was frigging *cold*!

Edgar was a ten-carat liar. All the time, while he was putting the blocks to me off-camera, he kept saying what a great star he was going to make out of me. But all he wanted was my pussy. I wasn't born yesterday.

Finally, I'd had enough. He comes to the studio in his custom stretch limo and the first thing he wants to do is screw me in his trailer before the morning's shoot. Told me he needed to release sexual energy. To relax his creative drive. Creative, my ass!

He'd been directing this moronic vampire flick, *The Devil Bat's Daughter*. I was the daughter, but natch I got snuffed in the first reel with my boobs hanging out.

I was really pissed. When we were inside his trailer that morning I put some stuff in his coffee. Gave him a heart attack. When he keeled over I started screaming for help. Terrified maiden with a dead director on her hands. Great scene. I was wonderful. Academy Award caliber.

Naturally, the doc couldn't do anything for Edgar. I sobbed up a storm. Big-time tears. The whole bazonga. The doc was so concerned about me that he gave me a prescription to calm my "severe emotional state." Hah! All the time I was giggling inside. The lecherous, lying bastard was dead.

I don't feel any guilt. Not a twinge. Hey, he killed his wife, didn't he? Poisoned her. That's where I got the idea for the stuff in his coffee—from the diary I fished out of the garden shed. When he was loaded one night in bed he kept mumbling the combination, over and over again, like a mantra. Didn't have any memory of it the next day—alcoholic blackout—but by then I'd written the numbers down. I'm very clever about things like that. Got a good head on my shoulders. Mama always said so.

And she was right about my talent. When Edgar had his "unfortunate heart attack" I started moving up the industry ladder. Took a while. I'm no spring chicken. And recently, as a "mature" actress, I started getting some fat parts with the likes of DeNiro, Stallone, and Sean Connery. (I was Connery's doped-out mistress in *Kill Me Sweetly*. A plum role. Won me a Golden Globe! Hotcha!)

They're calling for me on the set so I'll quit writing, but my jouranl is real important. Me writing to me. Very healthy. This no-bullshit stuff is supposed to flush out the emotions. Gets me ready to emote in front of the cameras.

In this one, the picture I'm doing now, I'm a bitchy killer. I drive an icepick into my boyfriend. The producer told me I was perfect for the part. He was right. Fits me like a second skin. I could grab an Oscar for this one. Oh, yeah! Little Linda is ready for stardom! (Funny thing, me having the same name as Edgar's dead wife.) Anyhow, I'm ready for the big icepick scene. Killing my boyfriend in this one will be a pleasure. Easy. No problem.

After all, it's not real life.

⟴

Killing Charlie

Killing Charlie

The first time Dot killed Charlie was in Oakland, across the Bay Bridge, at an amusement park. They had an argument and she pushed him out of their seat on the Ferris wheel. Charlie went crashing through the roof of the ticket booth below, and there was a lot of screaming, with people running around like headless chickens.

A week later, when Dot (back from a trip to our local Sure-Save store) opened our apartment door, there was Charlie, sitting on our big overstuffed sofa. He smiled at her.

"Hi," he said. "Hope you brought home some of those yummy frosted cinnamon rolls for me. I'm really in the mood for a frosted cinnamon roll."

"I thought you were dead," my wife said. Her legal name is Dorothy, but I've always called her Dot.

"Nope. Still alive and kicking," said Charlie.

"But I saw you smash through the ticket booth." She was staring at Charlie, standing there kind of frozen, still holding the sack of groceries.

"Yeah, that was quite a shock," said Charlie. "Kind of hurt when I hit the roof."

"I thought you were dead," my wife repeated.

"I *was* shook up," Charlie admitted. "Had me some busted bones. Broke my nose." He touched his face gingerly. "But everything healed fast and here I am, fit as a fiddle, back in my happy home."

"I don't want you here," Dot said. "This isn't your home anymore."

"Hey, now…let's us try to get along," said Charlie. He shrugged his shoulders in a way that had always irritated her. "I forgive you for pushing me off that Ferris wheel. What the heck…I'm willing to let bygones be bygones."

"Well, *I'm* not," said Dot.

She put the groceries down, walked over to the desk, took out a loaded .38, and shot Charlie in the head. He fell off our sofa onto the rug. There was a lot of blood.

"Have to buy another rug," Dot sighed. "This one will never clean properly."

She dragged Charlie out through the kitchen and pitched his body off the fire escape. He landed with a *plop* in the alley.

Another week passed—and when Dot opened the driver's door on our Buick Roadmaster, Charlie was in the back seat, curled up and snoring.

"Wake up, you bastard!" shouted Dot. "And get the hell out of my car!"

Charlie sat up, blinking. He scrubbed at his eyes and yawned big, the way a cat does. "I didn't have the apartment key," he said. "Must of lost it when I hit the alley."

"I shot you in the head," Dot declared. "And it's a three-story drop from our fire escape."

"Yep," nodded Charlie, rubbing the back of his skull. "Bullet messed up my head for sure, and I broke both legs in the fall. Took a while for things to mend, but I feel all chipper again."

We lived in San Francisco, a few miles from the Golden Gate, and Dot drove out to the middle of the bridge and made Charlie jump. From that height, hitting the bay water is like going head-on into a concrete wall. Charlie sank fast.

Dot watched until she was certain that he didn't bob back up again. Then she drove home.

Everything was fine for another week—and then Charlie sat down in the aisle seat next to Dot in the AMC Multi-Plex where she was watching a new war movie starring Tom Hanks.

"Hi," he whispered, patting her knee. "How ya doin'?"

"This is crazy," Dot whispered back. "I *saw* you hit the water. You never came up."

"I know," nodded Charlie. "And boy, was it ever *cold*! Brrr! I get the shivers just thinking of how cold that water was. Freeze the balls off a brass monkey." He chuckled at the old saying.

"How did you get here?"

"The tide washed me ashore," he said, keeping his voice low. On the screen, Tom Hanks was killing Nazis with a machine gun. "Had to buy a new suit. My other one was ruined, being in the salt water so long. My shoes, too. Had to pay for a new pair."

"I don't understand any of this," said Dot. "I keep killing you, and you keep showing up again."

"Guess I'm just mule stubborn," Charlie said. "Or maybe I should say I'm like a rubber ball. I keep bouncing back." And he chuckled again. "But I harbor no hard feelings against you."

"I don't give a damn about your feelings," Dot told him, causing the woman seated next to her to protest. The woman couldn't hear the dialogue with all their jabber.

Dot stood up. "C'mon," she said to Charlie. "We're leaving."

They walked out of the Multi-Plex and Dot pushed Charlie in front of a bus on Market Street.

"Dear God!" cried the distraught bus driver. "I *tried* to miss him, but he just popped up, right in front of me. I just couldn't brake in time."

Charlie was crumpled under a rear wheel.

"He's dead, that's for sure," said a sleepy-eyed cop who was on the scene.

The bus driver shook his head. "My first accident. Wow! I really clobbered the guy. This is not going to look good on my record."

"A lousy break," agreed the cop. His eyes were almost closed.

Dot was watching them from the doorway of Mel's We-Never-Close Drug Store. No one had seen her push Charlie in front of the bus, but her stomach was rumbling.

She bought a packet of Tums for her tummy from Mel, walked to the garage where she'd parked the Buick, and drove home.

Charlie was sitting on the apartment steps when she got there. He looked pretty beat up. His new suit was ripped in several places and the left coat sleeve had been torn off.

"How did you get here so fast?" Dot asked him, plainly vexed.

"Took a taxi," said Charlie. "Woke up in the meat wagon, and when it stopped for a red light, I hopped out and found me a cab. Lucky I had enough money to cover the tip."

"I don't want you here," said Dot.

"But I *live* here," he said.

"Not anymore," she declared.

Charlie looked sad. "Getting whacked in the street by a bus is no fun," he told her. "I need to lay down for a while."

"It's *lie* down," she corrected him. Then she sighed. "All right, come on up and I'll fix you some hot chocolate."

"Great!" said Charlie, following her inside.

Dot put a saucepan of milk on the stove to heat, then got a box of rat poison from the top shelf in the pantry. She poured it all into the saucepan, then followed up with a couple of heaping tablespoons of cocoa mix.

"Whew! This stuff is *bitter*!" exclaimed Charlie, making a face. He held out his half-empty mug. "What'd you put in here?"

"Rat poison," said Dot.

Charlie convulsed, then collapsed on our new rug. No blood this time. She checked his wrist.

He was dead, all right.

She dragged the body out to the stair landing, and was about to pitch Charlie over the rail when he sat up.

"Look," he said to her, "I've ignored a heck of a lot from you lately, but this is the last straw. That stuff tasted *awful*."

"I put in enough poison to kill a whole *house* full of rats," she said peevishly. "How come you're still alive?"

"Simple," said Charlie. "I'm immortal. Seems to me you'd of figured that out by now."

"What makes you immortal?"

"About a month ago I was down in the Marina district, kind of kicking back," he said. "Then I spotted this funky shop, just off the main drag. Dark little place. Musty. Full of cobwebs. With all kinds of weird stuff inside. Run by a freaky-looking humpbacked guy with one eye and a club foot. Asked me if I wanted to live forever, and I said sure, that would be swell. Cost you ten dollars, he said. Okay, that seems fair enough, I told him. Once I'd handed over the cash, he went to the back of his store and came back with a beetle."

"A *beetle*?"

"Scarab, actually. He told me that scarabs guarantee immortality. An ancient fact, discovered by some Egyptian guys. Took a dirty pestle, ground the scarab into powder, dumped the powder into a cup of root beer, and—Pow!—I'm immortal. All for ten bucks."

"That's ridiculous," said Dot. "I don't believe anything like that could ever happen in San Francisco."

"Well, it did," nodded Charlie. "But lemme get back to what I was saying—about that rat poison being the last straw and all."

"Go ahead," said Dot.

"My patience is exhausted," said Charlie. "I don't think you love me anymore."

"I *hate* you," snapped Dot. "Absolutely loathe and despise you."

"That's pretty darn obvious," said Charlie. "But the point is, I can't let you go on killing me the way you've been doing. It's ruining my clothes. And bottom line, it's really annoying me. So…"

"So? So *what?*"

"So I'm going to have to put a stop to it."

That's when I drove my pocket knife into Dot's heart. She gurgled and slumped forward, sprawling out along the landing like a big rag doll.

She was dead. And my wife is not like me. She'll *stay* dead.

I pulled the knife out of her chest, wiped it off against the leg of my pants (they were ruined anyway), and put the knife back in my pocket. It has nostalgic value—Dot gave it to me on my thirtieth birthday.

By now, I'm sure you know who I am. Well, gosh, isn't it plain as pie? I'm Charlie. Been playing a little word game with you. Just to prove I haven't lost my sense of humor, despite all that's happened to me. And since I'm going to live forever, I *need* a sense of humor.

I thought about me and Dot. Strange how quick a good marriage can go sour. I'd been convinced that, deep down, she still loved me. But I was wrong. Dead wrong. Ha! Ah, well…

I left our apartment building and took a cab back to the AMC Multi-Plex on Market. Bought a ticket to the war movie with Tom Hanks. I'd liked the part I'd seen with Dot.

Worth another look.

Mama's Boy

Mama's Boy

Following her again. Told not to. Warned not to. Restraining order on me. Can't get within a thousand feet of her. Can't talk to her. Can't go near her house. Can't do a lot of things I'd like to do. But we'll see what I can do. Don't let shitty cops tell me what I can do or can't do.

She knows me. Oh, yes! Scared of me. Thinks I'm crazy. Told the cops I was crazy. Got roughed up by them. Lousy damn cops! Weekend in jail. Smelly. Toilet backed up. Homos in there. Almost raped in the shower. Had to yell for a guard. Cold. Heater broken. Nearly froze my ass.

Promised I'd stay away from her. Did for a while. Now following her again. But being careful. Staying far enough away so she doesn't know I'm there. Watching her at night.

Standing on the grass outside her window. Watching her talk. Eat. Watching her laugh. Beautiful teeth. White as snow. Watching her tits.

Watching.

Following her to the studio in my car. Staying well back in traffic so she can't see me in her mirror. Going to her pictures. Sitting in the dark watching her on the screen. Feeling close. Smiling at her in the dark. So beautiful. So very beautiful.

Shrine to her in my Hollywood apartment. That's what the landlord called it once. A shrine. Posters from all her movies. Hundreds of glossy photos. Magazines with her in them. Lots of times with her on the cover. One with her in a thong bikini. Showing what she's got. Interviews with her. Some where she talks about her marriage. Divorced. How she never sees her ex-husband anymore. He lives in Kansas City with another woman.

Went through her garbage. Found notes she'd written. Lists. Letters to her she'd thrown away. Best of all, a pair of her torn panties. Black silk, with lace at the edge. Keep them in a plastic bag. Special.

See her movies over and over. Every one of them maybe ten or twenty times. Never get tired of watching her.

We're very close. Meant for each other. Destiny.

Found out what studio she was working for now. Article in the paper. Followed her from the studio. To her new house. Big place in Brentwood. White with a red tile roof. Climbed up there one night. To see her undress in her bedroom. Exciting. Neighbor reported me. That's the first time the cops grabbed me. She told them to keep me away from her. Has a loaded gun in her house. Threatened to shoot me. Awful. Hurts to hear things like that. Why does she hate me? All I ever do is love her.

Second time the cops came was when she got home from the studio and I was on her porch. Waiting for her. I love you I told her. You are so beautiful. And I love your tits. To jail that time. Gave the cops a phony name. Have fake I.D. Don't give my real name. Ever. To anybody.

Judge puts restraining order on me. My picture in the papers. Said I should be in a mental ward. Treat you like shit in those places. On probation.

Changed myself since then. Cut my long hair real short. Now wear sunglasses. All the stars wear them. Shaved my beard. Makes me look different. Stare at my face in the mirror and it's like somebody else is there inside the mirror. Hello, stranger!

I'm thirty. Not old. Feel like a kid, in fact. Don't feel thirty. Used to live with Mama after Daddy left. Just the two of us. Slept in her bed. It was neat until I had to go to school. Always hated school. Didn't fit in. Grade school terrible. High school terrible. Got punched a lot. Blood on my clothes. Called me a mama's boy. What's wrong with being that? Always loved my Mama. Maybe too much. Had a psychological exam once. Guy told me I was obsessed. Obsessive personality potentially psychotic. And other bullshit. That's all it is. Doctors bullshit. What do they really know about me? Just sit there spouting their crap. Can't see inside me. Nobody can. Deep inside. Real me.

No friends. Nobody to talk to. Don't trust people. Wouldn't understand the way I feel about her. Don't really mind. Like it being alone and thinking about when I'll see her again. Bet she thinks about me too. Whether she wants to or not.

Have a hunting knife. Long blade. Real sharp. After jail, for a little while, I was pissed. Ran the knife right through her photo. One where her tits show. She shouldn't of called the cops on me. But I forgave her.

Don't hold a grudge. Not in my nature. Usually keep the knife in a locked drawer. Don't carry it when I follow her. Can't. Not smart. If the cops found it on me I'd probably go back to jail.

Went into a Hollywood store where they sell movie star stuff and bought this statue of her. Just her head and shoulders—no tits. Put it on a little platform and got some colored lights to go around it. Looks great with the apartment dark with just her statue and the colored lights making it glow. Almost like she's there with me in the room. Intimate.

She made a record from one of her movies. A musical. Has eight songs on it. Real nice soft voice. Like an angel would sound. Know all the words to each song by heart. Play them over and over.

Hot today. Middle of August. She came out to her car wearing a light summer dress. Yellow, with flowers printed on it. Tight around her ass and tits. Exciting.

Followed her home. Had the knife in my car. Took it with me when I walked into her back yard and used it to pry open a window. First I cut the alarm wires. Know where they are. Don't want the cops coming to grab me again.

She's inside. In the den. Fixing herself a drink. Hate it when she drinks. Her face goes puffy and her hair and makeup get messed and she doesn't care.

Kicks off her shoes. Settles into the couch. Snaps on the news. Sits there in her tight yellow summer dress with her drink, watching TV. Nobody else in the house. Maid's day off.

I go up to her. From behind. Put the tip of the knife blade against the faint blue vein in her neck. (*My* blood!) Smile at her as she jerks her head up, spilling the drink. Her eyes are round. Scared. She's really scared.

Love you, Mama, I say.

Poems

The Final Quest

Here now, stand close, and let me weave
    A tale so eldritch you'll believe
Me mad. For never has been told
    This death-dark saga. Brave and bold
Was Arthur, bearing Britain's crown,
    A king of courage and renown.
Begat above a thundered sea,
    A just and stalwart lord was he.
In glittered armor, head to heel,
    He smote rogue knights with magic steel.

With Saxon blood upon his blade,
    He came from battle to a glade
Where demons did upon him cast
    A deep spell dark-designed to last
Ten thousand years or more they say
    Till Merlin came at break of day
And found his lord in sleeping death.
    Then blew upon his cheek a breath
Which waked him full. Cried out the king:
    "The Earth shall ever of thee sing!
I vow upon sweet Jesu's name
    That you shall never want for fame."
But Merlin sighed and bowed his head,
    His waxen face deep-marked with dread.
"This fame, my king, that you bestow
    Avails me naught where I must go.

For though I saved thee on this day
  From Old King Death there is no stay."
"Not so!" cried Arthur, fist raised high,
  "I say that Death Himself shall die!"
"But surely, Sire, you speak in jest.
  No chance have we in such a quest."
But Arthur gripped good Merlin's arm.
  "I shall not let thee come to harm.
Death shall not pluck thee from my side.
  To his dominion we shall ride,
And there, I vow, shall king meet king.
  An end to Death's long reign I'll bring!"

And so began, as legends tell,
  A quest for Death where he might dwell.
On horse, Excalibur in hand,
  With Merlin, searched they land to land
Across the world. And years did pass
  Until, one morn, within a mass
Of stone from which no shadow's breath
  Was cast, at length they found Old Death.
Two kings, both bold, did thundrous reel
  Together, crashing, steel on steel.

And, sad by, watching Merlin wept,
  Aware that Arthur would be swept
From out this life. That even he
  Could not prevail now in the lee
Of Death's dark power. Yea, hour 'pon hour
  The marveled conflict hotly raged,
For never had the world seen staged
  Such awesome clash of mighty wills.
And ringing from the sky-tall hills
  Was word of battle swiftly sown
From castle wall to hut of stone.
  From moor and meadow, mountain, plain,

Fast came they all to see Death slain
   By Arthur. Duke, serf-slave, and lord
Were dazzled by his blazing sword.

A day, a night, a week passed by
   Without surcease. O'er land and sky
These titans met in frighted clash
   Of arms, to hew and maim and slash
Each one in turn, while moons did wane
   And blooded sunsets redly stain
The earth. And even those long dead
   Themselves raised from their graves, 'tis said,
And stood, stark-boned in silent rows,
   To watch these fearsome, dreaded foes.

Until, at long last, it was done
   Incredibly, their knight had won!
And Death Himself was laid full out.
   Then, heavenward, the strangled shout
From Arthur's throat: "We'll have no more
   Of Death upon fair Britain's shore!"
But Death knew well the knightly code,
   And to victorious Arthur showed
A face of guile. And, from the ground,
   His voice a low and piteous sound,
He asked for mercy, loud implored,
   Till Arthur put away his sword
To help him stand. Then Merlin rushed
   Straight on, ash-eyed, his tone close-hushed
In Arthur's ear. He harshly warned
   That here all mercy must be scorned.

"This thing I cannot do, good friend,"
   Said he to Merlin. "For once bend
Our code, and it shall surely break
   And, with it, knightly honor take."

Thus, Arthur's fixed code could not yield.
    He laid aside his blade and shield,
While foul and fetid Death roared free.
    And not for all eternity
Would king meet king in such a fight
    As this. And Death, in turn, did blight
The world for his defeat. All died:
    E'en Arthur, Merlin at his side,
Sore-wounded now, his magic fled
    In this, their final leafy bed.

And later, all of Camelot,
    Knights of the Table Round could not
Evade that final darkling wood
    Where smiling, white-boned tall Death stood
Supreme. No further songs were sung
    Of chivalry. The knell had rung.

Dirge For a Muted Trumpet

Slow road
Goin' nowhere…
                Somewhere's
                Where you don't go.
Long road
Leadin' nowhere…
                Been there,
                I ought to know.
Dead road
Endin' nowhere…
                I got there
                Long time ago.

In January Rain

Outside,
        In January rain,
    Shape-haunted night
    Remakes itself…

        But here,
        In the cocooned wooden dark
        Of a small club on Ventura,
        The shadow-beat
        Of a bleeding blues guitar
        Laments
        Gone-lost loves
           And empty mornings.
        A sad-high voice
        Here walks the scales of loneliness.

    In flickered candle mouths
    And silent-waiting drums
        The heart-pulse strings
        Vibrate flesh
           Among the sea-eyed crowd.

        In a club on Ventura,
        A small club on Ventura,
In January rain.

God Bless!

After fifty years.
Bradbury at eighty.
    Almost thirty when I met him.
    Trips to Long Beach. Great food and jolly times on the Queen.
        Signings in the Valley.
        Many lectures. ("Follow your loves!")
Good letters from Ireland. The pool in Palm Springs.
A Houdini séance at the Magic Castle, and a bicycle at MGM.
    Disneyland.
    Late night sessions at the house in Cheviot Hills.
Dinners with Donn and Dennis and Herb and Mayor Tom.
    Wild times with Freberg—and a special night at the Nuart.
    Bradbury on television. ("We'll seed the stars and live forever!")
    Old radio with Vic n' Sade.
    Plays in Pasadena.
On the set with Something Wicked, and documentary evenings at
the Guild.
    Dandelion Wine in Fullerton. ("Green light, Doug, green light!")
    A 50th wedding anniversary at the Four Seasons.
The Halloween Tree at the Academy.
Fahrenheit 451 at the Colony.
The World of Ray Bradbury at the Coronet.
    And at a gallery with Joe M. (Painted metaphors!)
In Ohio, for the dedication at Bowling Green.
    Manuscript readings.
    Acres of books.
    The incredible cellar. (A lifetime of memories.)
    Tapes with Norman on a Note of Triumph.

Afternoons at the office in Beverly Hills, and a limo to San Diego.
    In Culver City with Logan's Run.
    Listening to new stories, savoring old ones.

A Wonderful Ice Cream Suit at UCLA.
Susan's wedding reception and fine champagne.
Galleys
and contracts.
Hugs
and handshakes.
And...*always*...much laughter.
After fifty years.
Bradbury at eighty.
God bless!

The Horror Writer

Shadow shapes,
swimming in fogged darkness,
razored teeth,
  slicing deep, releasing
  crimson heart tides.

Prowling beasts,
beneath a scything moon,
wild of eye,
  lust-hungry for the kill.

Demonic fiends,
claw-fingered, eager
to rend flesh,
  in blood-gored midnight feasts.
  Specter spirits,
summoned from gloomed grave, risen
from dank coffined earth
  to fetid life.

Witch, devil, ghoul,
the tall walking dead,
night companions all,
who join me at the keys,
  Welcome!

Welcome to my world!

Valley Heat

The Valley sizzles
        in late September.
I found a house,
        near Cass and Cavalier
        where
a child's round white beachball sat
in the heat-blistered yard
        like an abandoned moon
        in a sky
        of yellow grass.

American Journey

Driving the looped highway
    through cake-sliced mountains,
    cloaked with grazing trees.
Passing a rust-smoked snake of train, dozing
    silent, in Arizona heat.
Through snow-patched pine woods
    into Flagstaff.
And now
    the timeless, sculptured-granite country
    of New Mexico.
The proud Indian with scabbed lips
    on the street in Gallup,
    walking his straight-backed wife with blind eyes.
Government House in Santa Fe,
    three hundred years of history
    etched deep
    into adobe pores.
The La Fonda Hotel, dark-carved-wood shining,
    at Plaza's end.

Into the small New Mexico villages.
Old churches,
    with tilted wooden floors
    and blood-painted Christs.
Into Taos, dirt streets leading
    to the Pueblo beyond town
    and huddled rooftop women
    wrapped in blankets and silence.
Through a lush, tight-winding road,
    past high cathedral cliffs
    orange with westering sun.

To Raton,
>   and the dead hotel
>   at Colfax Junction,
>   adrift among piñon and juniper.

Into northern Texas,
>   through crumbling towns,
>   wind-scoured, flake-painted.
The hush of Easter morning
>   in Dealey Plaza, where Kennedy's ghost
>   still rides
>   the black death car.
To greener, softer Austin country,
>   a pink-domed capitol
>   alight in Texas sun.
To San Antonio
>   and the Alamo,
>   cannon-echoed, rebel-proud.

Louisiana, then, and New Orleans,
>   narrow night streets
>   loud with jazz and tourist laughter.
The shocked, sound-heavy
>   downrush of rain
>   in moss-draped Mississippi.
The swift run, sun-spangled, along the gulf,
>   with tall white pillared mansions
>   facing the shore
>   like landbound ships.
The sadness
>   of Southern Gulf cities,
>   their red bricks dark
>   with time's decay.
Caught in sudden-blinding
>   Alabama fog
>   outside Montgomery.
Into Atlanta, easy-rolling, thick-treed,
>   festered
>   by shingled, desolate acres.

To Greenville,
    North Carolina,
    and aimless good ole boys
    drinking canned beer
    in Friday-night cars.

Now along shiny asphalt roads
    past tall Colonial relics
    stirring images of musket fire and drum.
Past wedding-white plum trees
    into Old Salem
    and its new Yesterday streets.

To the wind-chilled Atlantic Coast
    and Virginia Beach.
Through sand-duned woods
    to the reaching
    steel-and-concrete finger
    leading to Chesapeake Bay.

Down the smooth-sliding run
    through Maryland
    and Delaware,
    into Washington D.C.,
    spacious, beautiful, violent.
To the endless row houses
    of Old Baltimore
    and thoughts of Scott Fitzgerald.

On, swiftly now, to the flat gray terrain
    of New Jersey.
Then the George Washington Bridge,
    bullet-shot
    into the clash and lion-loud
    clamor of New York.
And the final, unreal stillness of a quiet hotel
    at journey's end.

Imagine Him

(Remembering Raymond Chandler)

Imagine him,
　　with Cissy gone.
　　Fierce,
　　bitter-tongued and lost,
　　centerless
　　in a swollen, time-bent body,
　　death-mirrored eyes behind hornrims,
　　brooding,
　　iced-Scotch in hand.

Imagine him,
　　creator of Marlowe,
　　hard-muscled, hard-minded,
　　a tarnished knight
　　walking mean streets,
　　quick with wit and wisecrack,
　　the chess-playing lonely warrior,
　　kinetically alive,
　　forever young,
　　in rhythmed prose,
　　tilting at the windmills of crime,
　　a man on the edge.
　　Created by Chandler.

Imagine him.

Undead

I seek the night
     stalk with it
     down moon-silent streets
weaving through
     its spidered shadows
     deep-webbed
in midnight-sleeping towns.

I glide witch winds
     across
     vast ash-colored plains.
I feed
     on dreams
     on fears
     on sorrows
     stored secretly by day
but released to *me*
     in darkness.

I seek the night
     in red hunger
for how can my rich
     blood-dark dreams
     find substance
in the horrors of full day?

Avalanche!

The high white cry
    of the mountain
The snow-and-granite
    downrush
    of centuries
The stunned
    tumbled
    massive
    uprooted flow
    of forests
The cry of time and living rock
    gutted
    from the mountain's flank
    to fall
    into a final
    silk-white
    silence

Hemingway: Now Never There

The line sings out,
taut with balanced drops,
as great striped marlin run
in cold Gulf fathoms.
The corded strength that pulled them up,
bursting, cannon-loud,
from deep-foamed country,
is no longer at the line.
Papa is not there,
battle-proud, the sea eyes slitted,
brown scarred hands upon the rod
to fight them
from *Pilar's* flying bridge.
Not there.

Not there in green high grass safari country,
alive with lion and wildebeeste,
the strong-thewed Kilimanjaro hunter
stalking Serengeti plain
for lesser-great kudu,
brass shells ready in the breech.

Not there in old Madrid,
beyond the Prado,
where ripped-silk sounding
ghost artillery
freight-trains Spanish skies.
Not there in fields
of golden-blowing chaff
beneath the castled hills of war.
(*Que ta*, Papa?
 Que tal?)

Not there
in narrow, sun-danced streets,
where rush brave black Pamplona bulls.
Not there at the barrara,
where,
under pivot of hoof,
ringed sand spits up,
and curve of killing horn is met
by flourished crimson cloth.
Not there
as man,
all lemon and stitched silver,
conjures past the bulk of beast
in timeless ritual.

Not there
in thigh-deep wild wood waters,
trout rich
where he walked
invisibly,
in pebbled Colorado depths,
the pack tight-rolled,
the tent unslept in,
the campfire
ancient ashes on the shore
in cricket-speaking night.

Now waits the Alpine slope,
empty of his climbing boots,
snow-cold,
steep-rising to the Madlener-Haus.
No double line
of ski tracks trace
the fur-white mountain's downward plunge,
for Papa is not there.
Not there upon the slope.

Not there in many-columned Venice,
where Renaissance gondolas,
bearing lovers young as summer,
stir moon-etched liquid paths—
and marsh ducks cry
beyond the Grand Canal.

And not there where he fell,
a raw eighteen,
in nightmare shrapnel burst
at Fossalta di Piave;
no trace of Papa now,
no trace of boy or man.
The earth is bare of him.
His blood is dust
in Italy.

Not there on the rue Notre-Dame-des-Champs,
or at the Dôme,
or by the Left Bank in French-falling rain.
But…
once there,
when generations lost were found
and fine white wine was cheap,
when Scott and Gertrude reigned
with Cézannes at the Louvre,
and elm leaves drifted in the Seine.
When wars were yet unfought
in blood-barked Hurtgen Forest,
dreams, fresh-minted
there, then, in Paris
and with the horses at Auteuil,
but now, not there.

Not at Toots Shor's or the Stork,
or at La Floridita,

nor chasing sailfish
off Mombasa,
or boxing at Kid Howard's.

Not there in teeming Key West waters,
or in the Dry Tortugas,
or on the trails of Michigan
ablaze with autumn's firefall—
or in young Kansas City,
Toronto,
Oak Park,
the Cooke City ranch:
remembered places where he lived
and grew,
played baseball,
hiked,
made love,
read late into the gusting dark.

The breathing woods no longer
softly crackle
to his quick Indian tread.
No flushed quail rises,
beating air;
no cabin waits, warm-hearthed,
on Walloon Lake.
He is not there.

Not there at Finca Vigia
with Miss Mary,
pirate-proud,
mounted heads along the walls,
his books upon the shelves,
the cats to feed,
the writing to be done.

Not there, painfully standing,
bare-chest-bearded,
above scrawled words,
putting life to paper,
making his art,
telling it true and how the weather was.

The Finca waits,
love-haunted;
and waiting, too, the many places
of his world:
the churched woods,
the rioting rivers,
the dust-scrolled Spanish hills
and good Wyoming in the fall.
But Papa is not there.

Not there.
Now never there.

Teeth of Acid

Teeth of acid
 tear my flesh.
Young flowers bleed
 and worms of fire
  consume me.

Sticks

He sleeps,
        Root-deep,
In moonlight-marbled woods,
Snow-boned and stark,
        Some ivory sticks
        In tumbled earth.
Dreams are dust,
All hope ghost-vanished,
        Now…
                        Smiling
In his skull's long sadness.

Blade

The crescent moon
  slashes down
    stabbing through trees.

        The crescent moon
          is a blade
            cutting deep.

            The dark is wounded
              and bleeds black.

Into Vienna

Out of London's Victoria Station
    to the Devon Coast

The choppy waters of the English Channel
    on the crossing to France
    with wide-winged gulls
    like thrown confetti
    against the chalk-white Cliffs of Dover

Into the bright, boat-swarmed harbor
    at Boulogne

Skimming past summer-fresh countryside
    on the long, drowsing
    afternoon train ride to Paris

Into the City of Lights
    aburst with energy, rippling
    with the cross-babble of foreign tongues

The narrow, climbing streets of Montmarte
    and the tourist-rich cobbled square
    under the domed shadow of Sacré-Cœur

The thrusting, soot-dark gargoyle faces
    of Notre Dame

The smart, expensive, bright-awninged shops
    along the Champs-Elysées

The awesome splendor of Versailles
    with its golden rooms
    and marbled halls

The bitter-smoked steam engine
    pulling us, with panting breath
    out of the Gare de l'Est

The immaculate white tablecloths
    laid with dazzled silver
    in the etched-glassed dining car

The night trip through Germany
    with a hushed depot stop in Stuttgart
    a city asleep beneath the blazing
    three-pointed star of Mercedes

The morning run through Austria
    passing flower-decked cottages

Into the sun-blazed richness
    of Salzburg

Through the storied Vienna woods
    rising eternally
    in a rolling, green-black tide
    beyond the window

Crossing the Danube
    into fabled Vienna
    the *Third Man* city

With its under-street crypt
    bearing the silver-scrolled
    coffins of emperors

Into the Palace of the Hapsburgs
     and its vast, far-spreading
     formal gardens

To a concert hall alive with violins
     and into homeward darkness

With memories of Mozart
     currenting the steepled streets.

A Death Of Yesterdays

You stand
     ghostlike
     in my past,
reminding me
     that friends can die
     and not be dead,
     that life is not, oft-times,
     made up of mortal stuffs,
and that a death of dreams,
     of yesterdays
can be as real
     as coffined earth.

Norman At Ninety

The hair gone wild and white,
    Physically altered—but not in spirit.

No, never in spirit.

    Weathervane of universal morality,
    Implacable enemy of The Bomb,
    Celebrant of human aspiration…
      (Try, we must always try to be kinder, wiser, better)
    American patriot
    Engaged (and engaging) historian.

Holding forth for Liberty and the pursuit of,
    Dispensing Truth, applauding Justice,

A gentle man's gentleman.
Purveyor of decency
    Pundit and punster,

Ever vigilant against that
    which is trivial, demeaning, vulgar, and meretricious,

Whose singing words transcend a media,
Achieve nobility,
Speak to the cause of Common Sense—

    This Teacher of Eternal Verities,
      Soul-mover,
      Earth-lover,

    Ever stalwart in pursuit of
    That which is Moral and Proper.

We owe him much, this ageless man,
For words that burn and stir,
    Ideas that seed and cultivate
    The best in us. (He'll settle for nothing less.)

    Corwin at ninety.
    Value him.
    As he values us.

Wind Cry

Sun-splintered
Moon-struck
White linen
Wrapped in curve of feather
Hem-stitched in skyblue
Cloud-framed and easy-circling
Alone
Above wind-fisted sea
And blaze of beach
Crying
The lost child's cry
In feathered solitude
Seeking horizons
Dreaming wind dreams
Tilting at the world
That lives below

> The sand people shade eyes
> To see it
> Remarking on its voice
> How sad they say
> The gull's cry
> Sad for them perhaps
> Crying: Free!
>   Free!
>   Free!
> Forever—on a wind they'll never understand

Our Bond Is Darkness

Day is a brassing trumpet
Raging my ear,
A killing sound, knife-blading
My brain.
>Day is clangour,
>Confusion,
>And I am lost
>In the stab and sear
>Of sun.
Day is fierce,
Unforgiving,
A bright hot beast
Clawing my nerves.
>Day is my Enemy,
>And we shall always war.

>Night is a guttering candle,
>Soft-flamed,
>Laced with shadows.
>>Night is a panther's velvet back,
>>Cool with frosted moon,
>>Dusted with starshine.
>Night is a sighing guitar,
>Whose voice
>Rocks me, easing pain.
>>Night is calm,
>>Motionless,
>>A time for dreaming.
>Night is my Friend,
>And our bond is darkness.

United Kingdom

The pomp and glitter
     of the Queen's Guard at Buckingham Palace

The raw life of Soho
     in the twist of its night streets

The fog-damp gray stones
     in the Tower of London

The spacious sweep and majesty
     of Westminster Abbey

The high, slow-ticking presence
     of Big Ben

The Dickens-grimed docks
     along the Thames

The squared greens
     of Cambridge

The country-quiet churchyard
     at Meldrith

The vast steel arches
     of Paddington Station

The tree-wild solitude
     of Christie's "Greenways"

The narrow coach roads
     into Cornwall

The ancient charm
of Woodstock

The spreading splendor
of Blenheim Palace

The stolid medieval strength
of York

The Old World dignity
of Oxford

The liquid ease
of Shakespeare's Avon

The ghost-haunted terrain
of Dartmoor

The rolling, russet hills
sliced by hedgerows
and, always,

The deep-bound sense of history
breathing from London's stone pores.

Plunge

The night tide carries him
    Along neoned pavement, mirror-splashed
With evening rain, a thousand dazzle shapes
    In glittered pools beneath
    His moving feet,
Past strangers in grim multitude
    Their faces stone to him, passive-eyed,
Seeing him, yet not seeing,
    Not understanding
    His raw pain.

A father unknown. A mother's voice
    Knife-cutting him at ten, a lacerating wound
At twelve, and gone from her, into the streets
    At fifteen,
    Where
Moving with the hostile cats, feral and alley-quick
    To take his prey,
    To leave his mark in blood.

Her prediction realized. Lost and sleepless
    Into savage dawns. Aimless,
Each breath taken without hope. Under lonely moons,
    In ashed despair.
    No hope here,
    No better days, no nights to savor. Only
The uncaring city-rush, the empty
    Soul-lost streets.
    Until tonight.

A *purpose* now. A stride of certainty. A clear design.
    Past gleam-iced windows jeweled in rain,
    Past deep-mouthed traffic lights, and out

Away,
To a final structure, tall and fierce in cabled concrete,

A stretch of stone, high and arcing.
And him walking swiftly, center-bound,
The hammered rain ignored, the bay wind meaningless,
With shattered stars alive in depths unplumbed.
Now...
The cold iron rail, a muscled glide over, his brain alive
With sudden hope. At last,
The plunge.
The long dark waiting.
And him, drifting down, leaf-free,
To meet
His fathomed victory.

After The Thin Man

Old Hammett,
Moving from themes full spent,
With falcons found,
All murders done,
To fresh far places of the mind.
Mountain and imaged woods,
As yet unreached,
New paths
Untrod.

Again! Assault!
Rage at white space unfilled!
Each day
A blading agony
At what's unfound, unclaimed,
Unearthed.

Until at last,
With virgin wilderness of words uncharted,
The keys are stilled.
And marbled silence reigns
In the void of books
Unborn.

The Artist

The sky is red,
with blooded sun.
The patchwork hills
are stained.
See how their colors run!

Clouds are burning,
some already charred.
The fireman, Night, appears
all cool
and multi-starred.

The alabaster moon,
the artist of the night,
paints the sky
with silvered brush
all delicate,
a canvas filled with light.

Cat

I watched
      the watching cat
      swoop-tailed at the window

Intent
      on butterflies
      and quick
      black-hopping crickets

Watching there
      with flickered ears
      and crystaled
      Chinese-blinking eyes.

Final Exit

(upon the death of Sylvia Plath)

The dark yew tree
    Partnered with night
Slumbered her.

The mouthing rose
    Seeping its brows of blood
Soothed her.

Until life (O shock of waking!)
Swarmed finally free
    From her cell-walled hive
Of self.

For My Wife...

You stretch
  my mind
  my mental muscles.
You show me places
  I'd never known
  but go
  because of you.
You make demands
  creatively
  that I pridefully fulfill.
You demonstrate
  what goodness is
  and care
  for every creature.
You carefully move
  the sidewalk snail
  to safer ground.
You flood life's darkness
  with your light.
              Because of you
              I'm me.

Have You Seen The Wind?

Have you seen the wind bend the trees in storm?
Have you seen the lightning put out the stars?
Have you seen the rush of waters in full flood?
Then you have seen my love dancing.
Dancing, dancing, you have seen my love
  Dancing.

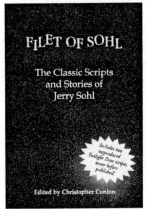

FILET OF SOHL

The Classic Scripts and Stories of Jerry Sohl

Edited by Christopher Conlon

ISBN: 0-9714570-3-4   **$16.95**

JERRY SOHL (1913-2002) was one of the most successful science fiction, fantasy, and mystery writers of his time. A prolific author of novels (*Costigan's Needle, Point Ultimate*) and films (*Die, Monster, Die!* with Boris Karloff), he is perhaps best-known today for his teleplays for *The Twilight Zone, Star Trek, The Outer Limits*, and *Alfred Hitchcock Presents*. This is the first-ever collection of this master's scripts and stories!

Included in this volume:

★ Ten classic short tales, including two adapted for the legendary *Outer Limits*
★ Two never-seen scripts for *The Twilight Zone*
★ An intriguing story treatment for *Alfred Hitchcock Presents*
★ A powerful foreword by William F. Nolan
★ Essay-appreciations from George Clayton Johnson, Richard Matheson, and Marc Scott Zicree
★ Touching personal tributes from the author's son and daughter, Allan and Jennifer Sohl

FOR FANS OF CLASSIC SCIENCE FICTION, FANTASY, AND SUSPENSE—THIS IS A BOOK TO SAVOR!

____ YES, please send me ____ copies of *Filet of Sohl* for just $16.95 each.

____ YES, I would like more information about your other publications.

Add $4 postage for up to 5 books. For non-US orders, please add $4 per book for airmail, in US funds. Payment must accompany all orders. Or buy online with Paypal at bearmanormedia.com.

My check or money order for $_____ is enclosed. Thank you.

NAME _____

ADDRESS_____

CITY/STATE/ZIP _____

EMAIL _____

Checks payable to: BearManor Media * P O Box 750 * Boalsburg, PA 16827
ben@musicdish.com

Have You Seen The Wind?

Selected Stories and Poems
by William F. Nolan

ISBN: 0-9714570-5-0   **$14.95**

With 75 books and over 300 anthology appearances to his credit, William F. Nolan (author of *Logan's Run*) is twice winner of the Edgar Allan Poe Special Award. Most recently, he accepted the International Guild's Living Legend Award for 2002.

This is the first collection of Nolan's horror fiction and verse to share a single volume. Six chilling tales of murder and madness, guns and obsession steam the pages of this haunting book, including "In Real Life," cited in *The Year's Best Fantasy and Horror*, and a brand new story written just for this collection: "Behind the Curtain."

Delve into Nolan's darkest worlds as he assembles tales of an ex-wife claiming revenge from beyond the grave… of an insane mind justifying the murder of his mate through the tall glass of a cold one… of a husband who refuses to stay dead… And top it all off with a celebration of this master's widely-praised poems, on topics ranging from Bradbury to Vienna, from Hammett to Hemingway.

COMMENTARY ON NOLAN'S PROSE

"William F. Nolan is a hell of a writer! I have real admiration for his stories."   —PETER STRAUB

"He makes a permanent dent in our memories. Nolan is able to create an atmosphere of ultimate terror, causing readers to live out his nightmares."   —RAY BRADBURY

"He's incredibly talented … Each of his stories is like a psychiatric session from which the reader comes away knowing more about the human condition, due to Nolan's fascination with the topography of emotional torment and his infallible rendering of the troubled psyche."
          —RICHARD CHRISTIAN MATHESON

AND ON HIS VERSE

"Nolan is a prime communicator … and although he writes only 'two or three' poems a year, he manages to communicate emotions better than most full-time poets."
          —SMALL PRESS REVIEW

___ YES, please send me ___ copies of *Have You Seen The Wind?* for just $14.95 each.

___ YES, I would like more information about your other publications.

Add $4 postage for up to 5 books. For non-US orders, please add $4 per book for airmail, in US funds. Payment must accompany all orders. Or buy online with Paypal at bearmanormedia.com.

My check or money order for $_____ is enclosed. Thank you.

NAME _____

ADDRESS_____

CITY/STATE/ZIP_____

EMAIL _____

Checks payable to: BearManor Media * P O Box 750 * Boalsburg, PA 16827
ben@musicdish.com